RAINTREE BIOGRAPHIES

Thomas Jefferson

Michael V. Uschan

RAINTREE
STECK-VAUGHN
PUBLISHERS

A Harcourt Company

Austin   New York
www.raintreesteckvaughn.com

Published by Raintree Steck-Vaughn Publishers, an imprint of Steck-Vaughn Company.

Project Editors: Sean Dolan, Leigh Ann Cobb, Gianna Williams
Production Manager: Richard Johnson
Designed by Ian Winton

Planned and produced by Discovery Books

Library of Congress Cataloging-in-Publication Data
Ushcan, Michael V., 1948-
Thomas Jefferson / Michael V. Ushcan
p. cm. — (Beginning biographies)
Summary: An overview of the life of Thomas Jefferson, from his early years on a plantation in
Virginia through his education and political career to his role in the American Revolution and
years as president.
Includes bibliographical refernces and index.
ISBN 0-7398-5676-6
1. Jefferson, Thomas, 1743–1826—Juvenile literature. 2. Presidents—United States—Biography
—Juvenile literature. [1. Jefferson, Thomas, 1743–1826. 2. Presidents.]
I. Beginning biographies (Austin, Tex.)
E332.79.U814 2002
973.4'6'092—dc21   2002017757

Printed and bound in China.
1 2 3 4 5 6 7 8 9 0 MID 07 06 05 04 03 02

Acknowledgments
The publishers would like to thank the following for permission to reproduce their pictures:
Cover, pp.4 and 5 Peter Newark's American Pictures; p. 6 Bridgeman Art Library; pp.8 & 9 Peter Newark's American
Pictures; p.10 Bridgeman Art Library; p.11 Mary Evans Picture Library; p.12 Bridgeman Art Library; p.13 Peter Newark's
American Pictures; p.14 Bridgeman Art Library; p.15 Grainger Collection; pp.16 & 17 Peter Newark's American Pictures;
pp.18, 19 & 20 Bridgeman Art Library; p.21 Corbis; pp.22, 23 & 24 Peter Newark's American Pictures; p.25 Bridgeman Art
Library; p.26 Peter Newark's American Pictures; p.27 Bridgeman Art Library; p.28 Corbis; p.29 top Peter Newark's
American Pictures.
Map by Stefan Chabluk.

Dedication
With love to Imari, Mikey, Madison, and Tahitia. Uncle Mike.

THOMAS JEFFERSON

July 4 is a special day for Americans. It is called Independence Day, because it was on that day in 1776 that the 13 colonies approved the Declaration of Independence. The colonies were fighting for their freedom from Great Britain in the American Revolution. The document explains why Americans had the right to govern themselves, and it was written mainly by one man—Thomas Jefferson.

By 1800, when this portrait of him was painted at age 57, Thomas Jefferson's red hair had turned gray with age. His intelligence and determination were unchanged, however. That year he was elected president.

RELIGIOUS FREEDOM

Jefferson fought for many kinds of freedom during his lifetime. In 1779, Jefferson introduced the Bill for Establishing Religious Freedom into the Virginia Assembly.

A Sentence That Changed the World

"We hold these truths to be self-evident, that all men are created equal...."

The Declaration of Independence

Jefferson did many great things. He was governor of Virginia and the third president of the United States. Jefferson was also a musician, scientist, architect, diplomat, inventor, and educator. At the end of his life, he declared that his three greatest achievements were writing the Declaration of Independence, founding the University of Virginia, and writing the Statute of Religious Freedom for Virginia.

Jefferson wrote the Declaration of Independence, one of the most important documents in U.S. history. It explained to the world why all people should be free to govern themselves.

GROWING UP AT SHADWELL

Thomas Jefferson was born on April 13, 1743. His parents were Peter and Jane (Randolph) Jefferson. He grew up on Shadwell, a plantation of over 1,000 acres in Virginia, near present-day Charlottesville. Thomas loved his father, who often went riding with him and taught him many things about farming and nature.

An early 19th-century depiction of a building on a Virginia tobacco plantation.

THE BRITISH COLONIES

In 1743, Virginia was one of 13 North American colonies Great Britain had founded during the 17th century. The colonies were located along the Atlantic Coast, extending only a few hundred miles west into the land that would one day become the United States of America. Beyond them was wilderness, inhabited primarily by Native Americans.

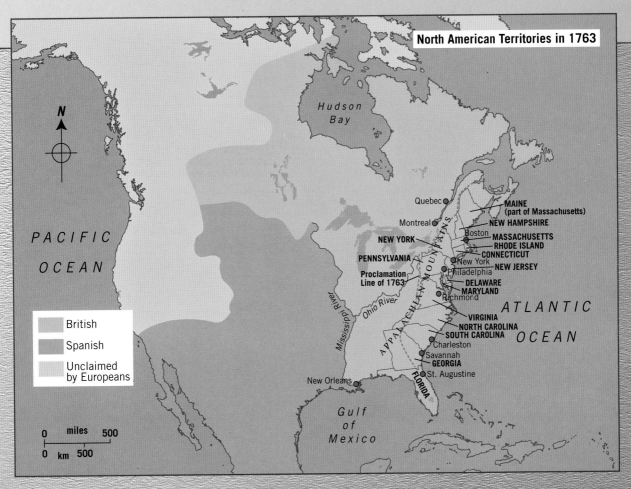

North American Territories in 1763

Hudson Bay

PACIFIC OCEAN

ATLANTIC OCEAN

Quebec
Montreal
NEW YORK
PENNSYLVANIA
Proclamation Line of 1763
Mississippi River
Ohio River
APPALACHIAN MOUNTAINS
MAINE (part of Massachusetts)
NEW HAMPSHIRE
Boston
MASSACHUSETTS
RHODE ISLAND
CONNECTICUT
New York
NEW JERSEY
Philadelphia
DELAWARE
MARYLAND
Richmond
VIRGINIA
NORTH CAROLINA
SOUTH CAROLINA
Charleston
Savannah
GEORGIA
St. Augustine
FLORIDA
New Orleans
Gulf of Mexico

British
Spanish
Unclaimed by Europeans

0 miles 500
0 km 500

Peter Jefferson died on August 17, 1757. The oldest child in his family, 14-year-old Thomas, was now head of a household that included his mother, six sisters, and a baby brother. This gave Jefferson a lot of responsibility at a very young age, and he was determined to make something of himself.

GOING OUT INTO THE WORLD

Thomas Jefferson was educated at home by tutors and then in local schools until he was 17. An eager student, Jefferson always learned as much as he could, even how to read the classical languages of Greek and Latin. In 1760, he entered William and Mary College in Williamsburg, the colonial capital of Virginia. Two years later, he quit to study law.

Jefferson attended William and Mary College, which began teaching students in 1693. This picture of the famous college was painted in 1935.

The Right of the People

Jefferson wrote: *"Whenever any form of government becomes destructive, it is the right of the people to alter or abolish it."*

The Declaration of Independence

PATRICK HENRY

One of the people who influenced Jefferson was Patrick Henry (below), a member of the House of Burgesses. Henry's argument that Great Britain was misruling the colonies helped convince Jefferson that they should govern themselves. In a famous speech, Henry said in 1775 that he was willing to fight to the death for America's freedom: "I know not what course others may take; but as for me, give me liberty or give me death!"

In 1767, Jefferson went to work as a lawyer in Williamsburg. Jefferson was interested in how government worked and began attending sessions of the Virginia House of Burgesses, colonial Virginia's governing body. He learned how legislators made laws. During this period, Jefferson also became convinced that the colonies should be freed from British rule.

LAWYER, HUSBAND, LEGISLATOR

In 1768, Thomas Jefferson was elected to Virginia's House of Burgesses. Two years later, he began to design and build a house not far from his childhood home. He called it Monticello—which means "little mountain" in Italian—because it was at the top of a hill. Over the years, Jefferson made Monticello into one of the nation's biggest and most beautiful homes. In 1773, he married Martha Skelton, a widow, and they had three daughters: Martha, Mary, and Lucy Elizabeth.

*Jefferson loved the beautiful home he lived in, which he named Monticello.
He designed it and kept making changes to improve it throughout his lifetime.*

This drawing shows a debate in the Virginia House of Burgesses against the Stamp Act, one of the many taxes that made colonists hate British rule.

Jefferson's first act as a legislator was to introduce a bill to allow anyone who owned a slave to free that man or woman, something not permitted then. The bill never became law. Although Jefferson owned slaves all his life, he said it was "an infamous practice" that should be ended. However, he could not see a practical solution to the problem of slavery.

FREE EDUCATION

Jefferson believed people needed to be educated to make democracy work. In his time, only rich people could send their children to school. He introduced a bill to create the first public schools that everyone, except slaves, could attend. He also introduced a bill for creating a public library. Both bills were defeated.

11

AMERICANS AND BRITISH RULE

The colonies that became the original 13 United States of America were founded by Great Britain in the 17th century. At first, colonists needed help from Great Britain to survive. This included protection from Native Americans and other colonists from France and Spain, all of whom also wanted control of American territory.

KING GEORGE III

George III (right) was king of England from 1760 to 1820. When the colonists asked for more freedom to make their own laws, he refused. Instead, he decided to force Americans to follow British laws by sending more troops to the colonies. He also introduced many new taxes that outraged the colonists.

Gradually these colonists, now calling themselves Americans, came to hate British rule. They wanted to govern themselves, because they believed many of the laws made thousands of miles away in Great Britain were unfair.

In 1774, Jefferson wrote *A Summary View of the Rights of British America*. In it, he pleaded with King George for more freedom for the colonies.

On the night of March 5, 1770, British soldiers in Boston, Massachusetts, fired on colonists who were taunting them, killing five Americans. The famous patriot Paul Revere made this illustration of the "Boston Massacre."

THE FIRST CONTINENTAL CONGRESS

The American Revolution began on April 19, 1775, in Massachusetts. On that day, colonists known as Minutemen, most of them farmers armed with hunting rifles, fought British soldiers (the "Redcoats") at Lexington and Concord. These untrained rebels held off the mighty British soldiers. The war that followed would be hard and dangerous.

THE BOSTON TEA PARTY

American opposition to British taxes increased in the 1770s. One famous incident was the Boston Tea Party. On December 16, 1773, a group of patriots, many of them disguised as Native Americans, destroyed a shipload of tea in Boston Harbor to protest the British tea tax.

Delegates from the 13 colonies met in Philadelphia in September 1774 at the First Continental Congress. The Congress condemned Great Britain for the way it treated the colonies.

The Tree of Liberty

Although war meant that many Americans would die, Jefferson believed it was worth the sacrifice. He once wrote a friend, W. S. Smith: "The tree of liberty must be refreshed from time to time with the blood of patriots and tyrants."

When the fighting began, Jefferson represented Virginia at the First Continental Congress. The Congress was made up of people, called delegates, from all 13 colonies. The Congress first met in 1774 to protest unfair British taxes and laws. When the American Revolution began, Congress became a legislative body that would govern a new nation—the United States of America.

WRITING THE DECLARATION

When the Second Continental Congress met in Philadelphia in May 1776, the Revolutionary War had been going on for one year. Congress wanted to tell the world why America was fighting for its freedom.

Thomas Jefferson, at 33, was the youngest delegate at the Congress. He was given the honor of authoring the Declaration of Independence because he was already considered one of America's finest thinkers and writers.

King or Tyrant?

"The history of the present king of Great Britain is a history of repeated injuries and [thefts], all having in direct object the establishment of an absolute tyranny over these states."

The Declaration of Independence

Thomas Jefferson wrote the Declaration of Independence in this Philadelphia house, where he rented rooms.

Thomas Jefferson (standing), Benjamin Franklin (left), and John Adams discuss the wording of the Declaration of Independence.

In mid-June, Jefferson sat at a desk and began writing one of the most important documents in U.S. history. Jefferson listed the injustices of British rule and explained why Americans believed they had the right to govern themselves. Jefferson was influenced by earlier documents on freedom such as the Magna Carta. But Jefferson's ideas were bolder than any that had ever been written.

THE MAGNA CARTA

The Magna Carta, or Great Charter, was granted in 1215 by King John of England. It was the first document to list basic rights that government could not take away from its citizens. Both the U.S. Constitution and that of every state have ideas and even phrases taken directly from the Magna Carta.

DECLARING INDEPENDENCE

Thomas Jefferson said he wrote the Declaration of Independence "to express an American mind." His boldest idea was that "all men are created equal." In Jefferson's time, kings and members of noble families were considered superior to other people. Jefferson also stated that everyone had rights that could never be taken away and that "among these are life, liberty, and the pursuit of happiness."

WHAT WAS LEFT OUT

Jefferson was not upset about most of the changes delegates to the Continental Congress made to the Declaration. But he was angry that they left out a paragraph in which he attacked slavery as evil and called for its end.

Delegates to the Second Continental Congress line up to sign the Declaration of Independence. They approved the Declaration on July 4, 1776, but they did not sign it until August 2.

Declaring Freedom

"We ... [declare] *That these United Colonies are, and of Right ought to be, Free and Independent States; that they are Absolved* [freed] *from all Allegiance to the British Crown, and that all political connection between them and the state of Great Britain, is and ought to be totally dissolved* [ended]. ..."

Declaration of Independence

Jefferson wrote that when a government tries to take those rights away, "It is the Right of the People to alter or to abolish it, and to [create a] new government."

The Declaration was approved on July 4. When it became public, it was hailed by most Americans, and the Liberty Bell, which hung in Independence Hall, was rung in celebration.

Independence Hall in Philadelphia was where Jefferson and other members of the Second Continental Congress approved the Declaration of Independence and made other important decisions about the American Revolution.

GOVERNOR, CONGRESSMAN

Thomas Jefferson returned to Virginia to apply the ideas in the Declaration of Independence. He was a member of the Virginia Assembly and then governor of Virginia from 1779 until 1781, the year the United States defeated Great Britain.

While governor, Jefferson was nearly captured by British troops: "A neighbor rode up full speed to inform me [soldiers were] ascending the hill to the house. I instantly sent off my family, and after a short delay, I mounted my horse; I went through the woods, and joined my family at the house of a friend."

At the Battle of Charlestown, South Carolina, in May 1780, the British were victorious, but the Americans would win the war a year later.

THE BILL OF RIGHTS

In 1788, while Jefferson was in Europe, the United States ratified [approved] the Constitution. Jefferson was unhappy that it did not list what rights people were guaranteed, such as freedom of religion. Jefferson and others persuaded Congress to add a Bill of Rights. The Bill of Rights became part of the Constitution in 1791.

Jefferson's wife, Martha, died on September 6, 1782. Jefferson was soon chosen as a delegate to the Continental Congress. He served only briefly before being sent as U.S. representative to France in May 1784. His greatest achievement in Congress was writing the Northwest Ordinance. This 1787 legislation created a system for new states, which allowed the nation to keep expanding westward. More importantly, it banned slavery from the Northwest Territory.

An Emerging National Leader

When Thomas Jefferson returned from France in 1789, he wanted to go home to Monticello. Instead, President George Washington named him the nation's first secretary of state, based on his experience, impeccable judgment, and knowledge of foreign governments. But Jefferson quit in 1794 because he disagreed with Treasury Secretary Alexander Hamilton and Vice President John Adams about their financial proposals for the "Bank of the United States." He thought the idea of a national bank was unwise, unconstitutional, and a threat to liberty.

George Washington was the commander who led the United States to victory in the American Revolution. In 1789, he was elected the nation's first president.

In 1796, Jefferson ran for president. He finished second to Adams, which in those days meant he became vice president. Because they were political foes, Adams ignored Jefferson for four years. A major issue dividing Jefferson, Adams, and Hamilton was the Constitution. Jefferson believed that the federal government did not have the right to do something unless the Constitution specifically said it had that power. His opponents claimed the government could do anything the Constitution did not specifically forbid.

FEDERALISTS AND REPUBLICANS

Jefferson was responsible for helping create the first U.S. political parties. Hamilton's followers became known as Federalists, and Jefferson's were Democratic-Republicans. Federalists generally believed in a powerful central government. Jefferson favored stronger rights for states and more individual liberty.

A PEACEFUL REVOLUTION

The 1800 presidential election was a strange one. The Republicans nominated Thomas Jefferson for president and Aaron Burr for vice president, while John Adams was the Federalist candidate for president. Adams lost the vote, and Jefferson and Burr tied with 73 electoral votes each. The Constitution stated that if candidates tied, the House of Representatives would choose the president. The House picked Jefferson, after more than a week of voting.

This picture of Jefferson was painted in 1801, his first year as the third president of the United States.

THE TWELFTH AMENDMENT

Until 1804, the person who became vice-president was the candidate who received the second-most electoral votes in the presidential election. In 1804, the Twelfth Amendment to the Constitution required that electors had to specify on their ballots who they were voting for as president and who they were voting for as vice-president.

In 1824, Washington, D.C., was still a quiet town on the Potomac River, yet it was the capital of a rapidly expanding nation.

Despite the closeness of the election, governmental power changed hands peacefully. The losing candidate did not call out an army or have people arrested. America's experiment in self-government seemed to be working.

On March 4, 1801, Jefferson was inaugurated as the nation's third president. He was the first president to take office in Washington, D.C., the nation's new capital, and the second president to live in the White House. Before 1800, presidents lived in New York or Philadelphia.

President Thomas Jefferson

R e-elected in 1804, Thomas Jefferson was president from March 4, 1801, to March 3, 1809. His most important accomplishment was to persuade France to sell its territory in North America to the United States. In 1803, for $15 million, America doubled its size, extending its borders west from the Mississippi River to the Rocky Mountains. The land—in what became known as the Louisiana Purchase—included all or parts of 15 states, including Arkansas, Iowa, Louisiana, Missouri, and Oklahoma.

In New Orleans, on December 20, 1803, the French flag was lowered and the U.S. flag was raised to show that the United States now owned the city as part of the Louisiana Purchase.

Freedom and Justice

In Jefferson's first inaugural address, he explained what he wanted for Americans: "Equal and exact justice to all men, of whatever state or persuasion, religious or political; peace, commerce, and honest friendship with all nations; freedom of religion; freedom of the press."

Lewis and Clark, during their famous expedition to explore the vast new land purchased by the United States from France. They traveled all the way west to the Pacific Ocean.

In 1804, Jefferson ordered army officers Meriwether Lewis and William Clark to explore the new, unknown land. Information they brought back helped lure settlers west. Jefferson played a key role in ensuring that Americans would keep heading west and eventually settle a nation extending from the Atlantic to the Pacific oceans.

During his two terms as president, Great Britain and France were at war with each other. Even though both nations attacked U.S. ships and forced American sailors to join their navies, Jefferson kept the United States at peace.

HONORING JEFFERSON

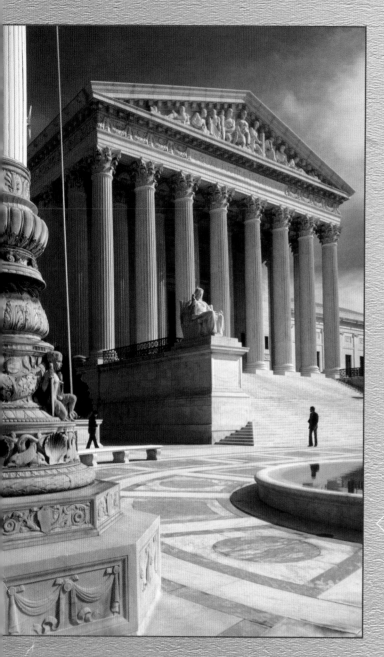

After eight years as president, Jefferson returned home to his beloved Monticello. He continued to read and study and helped found the University of Virginia. He died on July 4, 1826, the 50th anniversary of the approval of the Declaration of Independence. John Adams, his old friend and rival, died on the same day. They were the only two presidents who signed the Declaration.

The Library of Congress has more books than any other library in the world. The library's original collection was destroyed when Washington, D.C., was attacked by the British in 1814.

THE LIBRARY OF CONGRESS

One final monument to Jefferson is the Library of Congress, which has the biggest collection of books in the world. He established the library in 1800. In 1815, he sold some 6,000 books from his own collection to the library.

The Jefferson Memorial

The Jefferson Memorial opened on his birthday (April 13) in 1943. Carved on a wall of the monument, this quote from Jefferson expresses his lifelong defense of individual freedom: "I have sworn on the altar of God, eternal hostility against every form of tyranny over the mind of man."

Jefferson is one of the most famous and honored of all Americans. He is respected in many other countries because his ideas on freedom helped spread democracy around the world. He is one of four presidents whose faces are carved on Mount Rushmore in South Dakota.

Jefferson's image appears on the nickel, a fitting tribute since he helped develop the nation's currency, basing it on the decimal system. On the back of the coin is his beloved home, Monticello.

TIMELINE

April 13, 1743—Thomas Jefferson is born.

1760—Jefferson enters the College of William and Mary.

1768—Jefferson is elected to the Virginia House of Burgesses.

December 16, 1773—In a protest against a tax on tea, colonists destroy a cargo of tea in the Boston Tea Party.

April 19, 1775—Minutemen and the British clash at Lexington, Massachusetts, to begin the American Revolution.

July 4, 1776—The Continental Congress adopts the Declaration of Independence.

June 1779—Jefferson is elected governor of Virginia.

June 2, 1781—Jefferson resigns as Virginia governor.

October 19, 1781—British army, led by Lord Charles Cornwallis, surrenders at Yorktown, Virginia, ending the fighting in the American Revolution.

September 6, 1782—Martha Jefferson dies.

September 3, 1783—The Treaty of Paris between Great Britain and the United States officially ends the war.

May 14, 1787—Constitutional Convention opens in Philadelphia; delegates meet until September 17, when the Constitution is approved.

February 4, 1789—George Washington is elected president of the United States; John Adams is vice president; Jefferson becomes the first secretary of state.

March 4, 1801—Jefferson is inaugurated as the third president.

May 2, 1803—The United States and France complete the Louisiana Purchase for $15 million.

December 5, 1804—In the first election with separate voting for president and vice president, Jefferson is re-elected.

July 4, 1826—Thomas Jefferson dies.

GLOSSARY

Amendment (uh-MEND-muhnt) A change in the Constitution.

Bill of Rights (BIL-uhv-RITES) The first ten amendments to the Constitution.

Colony (KOL-uh-nee) A country or region that is governed by another country.

Constitution (kon-stuh-TOO-shuhn) The document that sets out the basic principles of government for the United States.

Continental Congress (KON-tuh-nen-tuhl KONG-griss) The first legislative body representing all 13 colonies.

Democracy (di-MOK-ruh-see) A form of government in which the people elect the officials who govern them.

House of Representatives (HOUSS uhv rep-ri-ZEN-tuh-tivs) The federal body of legislators elected from each state, according to its population.

Inauguration (in-awh-gyuh-RAY-shuhn) The ceremony in which a person officially becomes president.

Minutemen (MIN-it-men) Colonists who could get ready in minutes to fight the British.

Monarchy (MON-urk-ee) A system in which one person inherits power as the head of the government.

Native Americans (NAY-tiv uh-MER-uh-kuns) The first people to inhabit North America.

Patriot (PAY-tree-uht) An American colonist who opposed British rule.

Plantation (plan-TAY-shuhn) A large area of cultivated land, growing one staple crop and employing many people.

Redcoats (RED-kohts) A nickname for British soldiers because they wore red coats.

Revolutionary (rev-uh-LOO-shuhn-air-ee) Having to do with radical change or a change in government.

Senate (SEN-it) The federal body composed of two legislators from each state.

Slavery (SLAYV-uh-ree) A system in which people own other people and force them to work for no wages.

Tyranny (TYR-ruhn-ee) A form of government in which officials do whatever they want and citizens have few if any rights.

FURTHER READING AND INFORMATION

Books to Read

Jones, Veda Boyd. *Thomas Jefferson: Author of the Declaration of Independence*. Broomall, PA: Chelsea House, 2000.

Kallen, Stuart A. *Founding Fathers: Thomas Jefferson*. Minneapolis, MN: Abdo, 2002.

Lanier, Shannon. *Jefferson's Children: The Story of One American Family*. New York: Random House, 2000.

Santella, Andrew. *Thomas Jefferson: Voice of Liberty*. Danbury, CT: Children's Press, 2000.

Videos

Thomas Jefferson: Philosopher of Freedom, A&E Biography, 1996.

Thomas Jefferson. PBS Home Video, 1996.

Thomas Jefferson: A View from the Mountain. MPI Home Video, 1996.

Monticello: Home of Thomas Jefferson. Finley Holiday Film, 1996.

INDEX